Be The
Better Boss

Brian (Jack) Ash

For My Grandkids – Grayson, Bodhi, Sloane

To give them a head start in their careers should they wish to become the 'Better Boss'

What do you know?

You know what you know

Sometimes you don't know that you know

Many times you know that you don't know

What do you do when you don't know that you don't know?

Be The
Better Boss

A Simple Step-by-Step Guide to
Successful Management

By Brian (Jack) Ash

About the Author & This Book

Lacking a formal (college, university) education, Jack began his career as a rookie in a blue-collar environment but quickly discovered he had a white-collar aptitude.

Relying on mentorship and additional written material, Jack soon displayed a talent for problem-solving and creativity. His organizational and attention to detail skills resulted in promotions from mid-level to senior management (primarily in the hospitality industry).

In fast-based businesses (such as hotels), there can be a high staff turnover rate, causing hiring and training inconsistencies. Department managers spent more time putting out fires and redoing projects than managing.

Jack noticed and started handing out check lists to increase efficiency and consistency. Over time, these lists evolved to become the 10 step-by-step processes detailed in this book.

Jack realized these processes could be transferred to almost any business and would enhance the effectiveness and efficiency of business managers and owners. He soon developed a reputation as a startup and revitalization specialist.

Throughout the years of his career as a manager, owner and small business consultant, these processes have been time-tested.

Over many years, he has developed, participated in or written business plans, budgets, operations manuals, safety manuals, training manuals, build-out manuals, marketing strategies, promotional materials and computerized management systems.

Book learning is meaningful and valuable (i.e., manuals), but boots on the ground are where real-world learning is done. With the steps for each process, Jack has also included tips, suggestions and things to consider. Many of these are not found in standard instruction manuals.

Jack is a proud father, grandfather, writer and sometimes poet. He is a retired business manager and entrepreneur (The Boss) currently living in Dawson Creek, B.C.

Contents

You are the Boss - Now what?

Congratulations! You have decided to buy/start your own business (or have been promoted). You have agreed to join the management ranks – to be **'The Boss.'**

What's next?

You want to be a 'good boss,' but more importantly, a 'successful boss.'

You have questions: What kind of manager do I want to be? How do I get the staff to respect and listen to me? How do I know if I am making the right decision? How do I hire/train someone? What should I do next?

We have the solutions for you!

Did you know there are 10 main processes that every boss (owner/manager) will utilize in the day-to-day operation of their business? For each process, several steps need to be completed.

In short, easy-to-read segments, we will guide you through all the processes, steps, nuances and suggestions you need to keep you on the right track.

Implement these steps into your daily routine, and your stress levels will significantly diminish. Your confidence will soar as you make the right decision after the right decision.

You will become a **'Better Boss,'** and your staff and company will thank you for it!

How we can help

In a busy, fast-paced environment, who wouldn't want a quick reference guide filled with detailed steps, tips, nuances and subtleties that will give you the heads up on being a better boss?

Different skills are required, from department manager to senior management to small business ownership. The larger (more employees) the company, the greater the need for knowledge, consistency and efficiency in performing duties from staff and management.

Life can throw all kinds of curve balls at you, but if you have a basic understanding of what steps need to be done and in what order to do them, you can significantly improve your success rate, diminish your problems, reduce your stress levels, give more free time and gain confidence in your performance,

This short book will guide you, using stories, examples, tips and suggestions (in plain and simple language) through the necessary steps to help you be a better boss. And, of course – improve your lifestyle and make you more money. Now, who doesn't want that?

Although it is primarily presented for the business owner or manager, you will also find this information beneficial in your personal life. The processes, such as communications, projects, problem-solving or decision-making, are situations we face in our daily lives.

Before we get into the details, I want to introduce you to Bob and Mary. Bob works for a small 4-person company that makes and sells widgets. The owner is retiring and is allowing Bob and his partner, Mary, to buy the company.

They have been told about this program and requested our help preparing them for their new management roles. They will be arriving shortly for their first meeting with us.

John, one of our best associates, is going to conduct the session.

If you have a few minutes, why don't you join us as we give them an overview of the knowledge we provide?

Let's Get Started

Make us a Coffee

Bob turned off the main street into a small common shopping area and slowly drove between the four 2-story buildings. Spotting the signage for the 'Small Business Association,' he pulled into a designated parking spot.

As he unbuckled his seatbelt, he nervously looked at his wife, "Well, Sweetie, you still want to do this?"

Mary smiled and said, "Barb said this would really help us, so let's see what they have to say."

Before he opened the door for Mary, Bob tugged his tie and adjusted his sports jacket. Being a blue-collar worker, he was not used to wearing a tie and jacket, and they were snugger than he remembered.

The receptionist greeted them when they came through the door, "You must be Bob and Mary – John is expecting you, so if you follow me to the boardroom, I will let him know you are here."

They followed her to a small conference room. Inside was a round table and chairs for six people. A whiteboard stood to one side. In the corner was an 'L' shaped counter with a coffee machine and fixings neatly placed nearby. A couple of motivational posters and a calendar were hung on the walls.

Bob and Mary had barely sat down when a slim, average-height, silver-haired man entered the room. No suit jacket, no tie, his sleeves rolled up and wearing blue jeans – Bob liked him already and immediately felt more comfortable.

Smiling, he stretched his hand forward and offered a firm handshake to each of them. "Good Morning, Mary, Good Morning, Bob, nice to meet you – I'm John, and I will be helping you today."

John moved around the table and sat in a chair opposite them. He placed three small binders in front of him. Noticing Bob seemed a little nervous, John leaned forward, placing his forearms on the table and gave a small chuckle, "Don't worry, Bob – there are no forms to fill out and no exams. These are just the written materials we will cover in our sessions, so you can review them when you get home. Therefore, you don't have to worry about keeping notes."

Then John established eye contact with each of them. He asked, "Why don't you tell me a little about yourselves and why you are here today?"

Obviously nervous, Bob and Mary looked at each other – unsure who should speak first. Mary took the initiative and said, "We are buying a business, and our Financial Advisor suggested we talk to you first. She said that following the guidance and information you give us will greatly increase our chance of success and help make our company more profitable. We have worked hard for this opportunity and want to do whatever is necessary to improve our chances of success."

John turned his attention to Bob. "You look uncomfortable, Bob. We are very casual here, so why don't you take off your tie and jacket, relax, and tell me about the business you want to buy?"

Looking relieved, Bob did as requested and immediately felt at ease. He cleared his throat and began, "I work in production for a small 4-person company that makes and sells widgets. The owner is retiring and is allowing me to buy the company. I will run the operations, and Mary will take over the accounting and business end.

John nodded, "That's great! To be clear, you understand that we don't teach stuff like making business plans, accounting or how to make better widgets. Our goal is to inform you about all the little things that will make you a better boss – the steps, nuances and insights they don't teach you in class but are learned through years of experience.

Bob responded, "Yes, that was our understanding. I have been working for the company for eight years now. The owner is staying available until I get comfortable running the operations. Mary has a business degree and accounting experience."

"Tell me," John asked, "Have you ever hired someone, trained anyone, designed a marketing aid, or maybe dealt with an upset customer?"

"Not really, but I guess I will at some point."

"And that's what we can help you both with. We will show you and explain the steps you need to take to handle these situations. They will reduce your stress levels and increase your odds of doing things right – the first time. Are you ready for us to show you an overview of what you can here for?"

Receiving approval from each of them, John took 2 of the folders in front of him and handed them to Bob and Mary. Flipping his front cover open, he signaled them to do the same.

"Look at this list of the 'Processes' we will cover. Most of them are self-explanatory, but do you know the 'Steps' in each 'Process' that need to be taken and why"?

1. Communication Process
2. Decision-Making Process
3. Management Process
4. Leadership Process
5. Problem-Solving Process
6. Selling Process
7. Project Process
8. Hiring Process
9. Training Process
10. Motivation Process

John waited while they read through the list. Noticing the blank look on Bob's face, John smiled, "Don't worry, Bob, I know this might look complicated, but I promise I will make it easy for you and explain it in straightforward and easy-to-understand terms. I bet that just by looking at the list, you already recognize many items as parts of usual business operations.

For example, have you ever got a new book shelf or toy you had to assemble? Then, when you read the instructions, you find them less than helpful. Many appear to have been written by someone who had trouble translating between two languages or by a technician who used too many technical terms. They made your job much more complicated than it should have been, right?

Our approach is different – We understand that most people do not like to study or read manuals, so we will give you this information in plain and straightforward language, using examples or stories whenever we can to help you understand what we are telling you. Our program is not tailored to your specific business – it can be used by anyone in any industry or management level.

Do you have any questions so far?"

Bob looked over at Mary. She shook her head. "No, I believe we are both good; let's continue."

John smiled, "Alright." Let me explain what a 'Process' is and why we need to understand them."

Then John stopped talking and picked up his coffee cup. He looked inside and noticed it was empty. "But first, I think I would like another coffee – how about you, Bob – Mary." Both nodded that they would also like one.

John grinned and pointed over to the coffee maker on the counter. Looking directly at Bob, he said, "Great, how about you make us a pot"?

Startled, Bob leaned back in his chair and stammered, "Well, I...I...I have never seen a coffee maker like that – I don't know how!"

John chuckled, "It is OK, Bob - we will help you." He then picked up the office phone, "Joe, would you come to the boardroom, please? We need some help."

Moments later, Joe walked into the room, "What do you need, John"?

"Bob wants to make a pot of coffee, but he doesn't know how – will you please help him out."

Joe signaled his agreement and motioned for Bob to follow him, "Come on, Bob, let us make some coffee." He then waved to Mary, "Why don't you join us?"

Once Bob and Mary were in a position to see what he was doing, Joe listed the steps to be done – pointing to each area as he explained what he was going to do.

1. Check to see if the water chamber is empty

2. Use the pitcher to add water up to the level of cups you want to make

3. Remove the basket

4. Put in the filter

5. Add coffee to equal the same number of cups of water

6. Put the basket back in

7. Make sure the coffee pot is empty and clean

8. Place under the basket

9. Push the ON button

"Are you with me so far? Do you have any questions?"

Both Bob and Mary signaled that they understood and had no questions.

"Great, now watch carefully, and I will show you how it is done."

With that, Joe started from the beginning – this time slowly actually performing the tasks. – Except pushing the blue button.

"Well, Bob, do you think you know how to make coffee now," Joe asked?

Bob answered, "I think so; it looks pretty straightforward."

Then, to Bob's surprise, Joe removed the basket from the coffee machine, emptied the coffee back into the tin, put the filter back on the pile, and poured the water back into the jug sitting on the counter. He then waved his hand toward the machine.

"Wonderful – then show me how to do it."

With Mary and Joe watching him, Bob slowly went through the steps Joe had shown him. When he reached the last stage, he turned toward Joe, "Should I push the blue button?"

"What do you think? Did you follow all the steps? How about we go over it again, and you tell and show me all the steps you did?"

Bob retraced his steps, telling Joe, while pointing to each part, as to what he had done. When he was finished, he declared, "Yep, I did them all!"

Joe gave him a light pat on the shoulder, "Well done! Push the button!"

Bob's face broke into a big smile, and he playfully pushed the big blue button.

"Thanks, Joe," John said, "Much appreciated!"

A few moments later, as they were sipping some of Bob's freshly brewed coffee, John grinned and asked Bob, "I'll bet when you came here today, you weren't expecting to learn how to make coffee – did you?"

Bob laughed. "No, I sure didn't!"

John leaned forward, "I also bet that you don't realize what else you and Mary learned today."

Bob looked puzzled, and Mary just shook her shoulders. "What do you mean?" Bob inquired.

"Look down at #9 on the list of Processes I gave you. You have just learned the '**Training Process**' of which there are 4 steps:

1. Tell Them
2. Show Them
3. Let Them
4. Review

"Do you remember how Joe went about it – he told you the steps to take, then he showed you what he wanted you to do, then let you do it and finally reviewed with you what you had done."

John paused for a moment and let it sink in, and then he continued, "Not only training, but we also briefly touched on some of the other processes as well" -

1. Management – Identified a need/desire

2. Motivation – we were thirsty

3. Problem-Solving – No coffee in the pot

4. The Project – Make coffee

5. Leadership – Find someone to do it

6. Hiring – I asked Bob – but he had no experience

7. Decision Making – fumble through it or find someone who knows how

8. Training – Brought in someone with the expertise

9. Communication – Explained to Joe what we wanted to be done

"This was a simple example, but I hope it helps you understand how we are trying to help you. Of course, when running a department or managing a business, there are many more steps in each process. Still, when followed, they can make your job and life much less complicated."

John turned to Mary, "What is your impression so far?"

She laughed and gave Bob a playful pat on the shoulder. "Well, I'm delighted he finally learned how to make coffee! I have never been in management before and never thought about all these different processes. I am really looking forward to learning more."

"That is great, Mary! I know you and Bob are partners in the venture, and I believe you should also be involved in this learning process. Following the same steps in each process reduces potential problems or miscommunication. Not only that, but it will be much easier to cover for one another should the need arise."

"Bob, what are your first thoughts about what you have heard so far?"

Bob pondered his response carefully before answering, "I really like my boss, and he has been very helpful and encouraging. He is also very set in his ways, doesn't like change, and has resisted updating some of his procedures or equipment. Being inexperienced in some management aspects, I am beginning to understand how this program can help me. I'm ready to go to the next step."

John leaned back and smiled, "I am delighted to hear that, Bob. I have been watching both of you during our time today and think you both will do really well in your new venture.

Take your folders home with you and bring them back next time. After each session, we will give you a written copy of what we have covered.

To provide a foundation for future sessions, we have included some preliminary information that will only take a few minutes to read. It will help you understand why you need to know what we will cover.

Next time, we will get into the processes. All of them are important, but you will use some regularly and others you will only use once in a while.

We believe the 'Communication Process' is the most valuable and the one you will use daily. We will cover this in detail in your next session. You will never look at a conversation the same way again! I know you will find it most informative and exciting."

Then John shook their hands, and as he walked them to the door, he chuckled and remarked to Mary, "Remember, if you don't bring your own coffee, Bob now knows how to make it."

Some Points to Ponder

After supper, Bob refilled his coffee and headed for his favorite spot on the couch. Mary opens her folder and begins reading the information that John had given them.

After a few moments, she pauses and looks over toward Bob. "If I asked you what you do for a living, what you say?"

Bob replied, "I would say I make and sell widgets – why do you ask?"

"Well, it says here that you would only be partially correct," Mary retrieves Bob's folder from the kitchen counter and hands it to him, "This is quite interesting; I think you should read this too, so we can discuss it before our next meeting.

Bob nods, opens the folder and begins to read.

What do you do for a living?

Most people, when asked, will reply with a generic answer – "I'm a manager at Joe's dealership," "I own Ralph's Repair Shop," or "I run the Craft Store."

They are only partially correct. They have identified where they work and their title but not what they actually do. They are 'PROBLEM SOLVERS.'

Customers come to you because they have a problem, and they want you to solve it. For example –

Problem: We are hungry. Solution: Feed them

Problem: My 'Thing-a-ma jig is broken.' Solution: Fix it

Problem: I need a 'Whatcha-ma-call it.' Solution: Sell him one

Problem: I want something like this, can you make it? Solution: Build it

Now that you know the customer's problem, do you know what steps to take to solve the issue?

Can it be solved immediately, or will it take a while? Do you handle it yourself or assign it to a staff member?

How well you solve their problem can be the difference between a returning customer, who promotes your business, and an unhappy customer, who never returns. We will explain this in greater detail in the Problem-Solving Process.

You will do many different jobs as an entrepreneur running a small business. You may be an expert widget maker, but you will also have to be an information keeper, a purchaser, a salesperson, a planner, a problem solver and a fortune teller. One of your most important jobs is to be a 'decision-maker.'

The worst thing you can do in business is to make no decisions. Your company will have no direction, employees will become demoralized, customers become unsatisfied, and you will become frustrated and depressed. To make good decisions, you need to know the pros and cons of each situation. The processes contained herein will guide you toward making more suitable decisions.

There is an old saying, 'I must hurry for there they go without me, and I am their leader.' Without proper supervision and direction, staff will eventually digress into their own way of doing things – which may not meet your standards. Successful companies have good leadership. We will show you the steps to help you become an effective leader.

The most destructive force in business is poor communication. No matter what business you are in, your ability to communicate effectively will have a great deal to do with your level of success.

How will this knowledge benefit you?

You will better understand why you need to take specific steps (in each process) in the correct order because if you know 'why.' you will recognize the importance of what you are doing. That, in turn, will justify the effort you put into it.

By following these simple processes, you will find these things happening:

1. Sales go up (more happy customers)

2. Expenses go down (more profits for you)

3. Less stress (fewer problems to solve)

4. Correct decisions are easier to make

5. More discretionary time (time to do what you want to do)

19

Would you prefer to be planning for the sales you will make tomorrow or fixing the mistakes made yesterday?

Unfortunately, many people are in such a hurry to get where they are going they do not take the time to plan the trip. As a result, they get lost, sidetracked or derailed.

One of the most important things to remember –

If you do not have the time to do it right the first time – when will you have time to do it over?

How often have you heard – 'If you want it done right, you have to do it yourself'?

Is this because most employees or associates are incompetent? Or is it because a manager has not taken the time to train someone properly or does not even know how to teach them?

Initially, a good idea and lots of enthusiasm will get you started. Unfortunately, too much confidence can get in the way of sound judgment. When you first get into business, it is easy to become overwhelmed. Everything seems to be happening at once. Questions need to be answered. Problems need to be solved. Nothing ever seems to get done on time!

Our information will help slow you down so that you do things right the first time. It will help you understand how a good manager thinks. It will guide you through what shortcuts you should or should not take. It will walk you through the different processes to help you make correct business decisions.

In short, it will help you make money, help you save money, help you avoid or solve problems and, just as important – it will save you time - time to relax, time to plan for the next step and time to do what you want.

The biggest fear most of us have is to attempt to do something we do not know how to do. Even when someone gives us good advice, we often ignore it. Why? Because most of the time, we don't see why we should follow the guidance. We do not understand.

No one person can know everything. Those who realize this learn what they can then surround themselves with people with the needed skills.

Managers get busy with daily issues and may get lax in other areas. Memories fade, and details can get forgotten. Responsibilities may be handed off to other managers or staff who may not be fully trained, and shortcuts are taken. Over time, staff performance, production levels and customer satisfaction may decline.

All of us become lost time-to-time! We get so busy multi-tasking we can lose focus on what we are working on. Go back and review this material. Our step-by-step guidelines will get you back on track and ensure you do not miss any essential steps.

We recommend you periodically refer to the 'Process' sheets at the end of this material. Post them on your office wall or put copies in your desk drawer if feasible. For quick reference, take photos and keep them on your phone.

Not only will it comfort you that you are following all the steps, but staff will recognize you are following a plan and may also follow the steps!

1. The Communication Process

What Did You Say?

John was already sitting at the table with Bob, and Mary entered the room. Mary was wearing slacks, a summer blouse and a light sweater. Bob had switched to blue jeans and a casual shirt with an undone top button. He was smiling and obviously more relaxed.

Once they were seated, John took a deep breath and began babbling.

"Good morning nice to see you did you read the material I gave you I was talking with Jack this morning regarding the order of how we should present the process to you, and because you are buying an existing business, we should leadership first and selling second but I told him even though selling was important you already had a customer base and I thought we should concentrate on what kind of manager you want to be He disagreed and said because the owner was staying on for a while and could help you with the decision-making process that it should a lower priority and maybe we should start with developing communication skills instead what do you think?"

John stopped and took a deep breath. He looked back and forth between Mary and Bob a couple of times. "Well, what do you think," he asked?

Receiving only blank stares, he paused and asked, "Did you understand anything I said and what I was asking your opinion on?" Both Bob and Mary shook their heads.

John smiled, "That is why we will talk about good communication today. I was talking and telling you information, but not in a way you could comprehend. Talking and being understood are not the same things.

I misunderstood what you said.

Fluent English is not always the first language for many people. Levels of education, geographical accents or trade experience can directly affect a person's understanding and comprehension."

Sometimes, how you say something, rather than what you say, can significantly confuse someone as to what you really mean.

Handing each of them a sheet of paper, John continued, "Here is the same sentence written five times with a different word underlined each time. Please read each sentence out loud and place an emphasis on the underlined word. Bob, you read the first sentence, and then Mary, you read the second one.

1. **I** did not say he stole money

2. I did not **say** he stole money

3. I did not say **he** stole money

4. I did not say he **stole** money

5. I did not say he stole **money**

After they took turns reading the sentences, John inquired, "Did you notice the subtle differences?"

1. In the first example, the person is claiming innocence. It was not "**I**" but **someone else** who said he stole money.

2. In the second example, the person declared that they may have **thought** it but did not **say** he stole money.

3. In the third example, the person denies that they said **he** stole the money. The money was stolen, but not necessarily by him.

4. Example four alleviates guilt. He may have lost, miscounted or borrowed the money, but the person is not implying that he **stole** it.

5. In the last example, the identity of what was stolen is in doubt. It may have been supplies, food or clothing, but not necessarily **money**.

It is the same sentence with five completely different meanings. Most of us do not realize how our facial expressions, tone of voice or emphasis on certain words can significantly affect the message we are trying to get out.

Let's get into the details and see if we can overcome some miscommunication issues.

Communication Process

1. Present Idea

2. Understanding

3. Agreement

4. Trust

5. Harmony

1. Presenting your Idea

When you are ready to present your idea, try finding the time and/or place to eliminate (or at least minimize) outside interruptions. The more complex or involved the presentation is, the more important this issue becomes.

Follow the guidelines as taught by Toastmasters on giving a speech –

Tell them what you are going to tell them,

Tell them

Then tell them what you have told them.

In other words, start by giving them a view of the big picture, then slowly add in the details and then provide a summary of what you have been discussing.

2. Achieve an Understanding

Naturally, a one-sentence directive is less likely to be misunderstood than a twenty-minute presentation. However, if the person is not paying attention, is not knowledgeable in the subject matter, or fails to understand what is required, then there exists a potential for error.

If possible, determine the knowledge level of the other person(s) before you present your idea and then adjust your presentation (simpler language, more detail, and slower pace) accordingly.

Watch their body language – if they have a puzzled look, a blank stare, fidget, avoid eye contact or make a gesture that insinuates they want to speak – for signs that they may not have understood what you have just said. At this point, stop. Until you address the reason, everything else you say from this point on is not being fully heard. Ask the person, "do you have a question?" or "do you understand?" If they are 'lost' or do not understand your point, the impact of any additional information is lost.

Sometimes, it may mean reviewing the material, using different examples or plainer terminology. If they do not understand what is being proposed, wanted or required, you can bet that it will not be accepted, followed correctly and may have to be done over.

3. Getting an Agreement

Just because someone understands your presentation does not necessarily mean they agree.

Listen to all the questions and objections carefully. The only thing it will cost you at this point is a little extra time, and the benefits could be advantageous. They may have spotted something you missed or be aware of problems you may not have considered. They may know how to do it faster, cheaper, more simply or improve quality.

Should you already have considered or rejected some of their ideas, do not belittle them or quickly dismiss their observations. Acknowledge the suggestion, explain why it was denied or take it under advisement. An example would be – "That is a good idea; we considered it but decided not to because...." Or "We hadn't thought of it that way; let us think about it and get back to you."

By listening, you will enhance your reputation, appear more open-minded to suggestions, and demonstrate respect for the other person. Even if none of the tips are used, the other person will know you have at least considered their opinion. That alone will make for a more favorable relationship in the future. You never want to stop the flow of ideas or suggestions. You just never know who will come up with the million-dollar idea.

Once all objections, concerns or suggestions have been dealt with, you need to get a commitment of agreement from everyone involved.

For a simple task, this may be achieved by simply asking, "Are we in agreement?" or "do you agree?"

More involved projects may require a summation of the critical points, a verbal agreement and/or a written follow-up.

If there appear to be any doubts about the other person's understanding or agreement, then have them repeat the information to you. If anything is incorrect, now is the time to address it. If everything is correct, you can confidently say, "Good, we agree."

4. Trust

Trust builds between the parties involved once everything is understood and agreed to. Trust that it will be done correctly, on time and to everyone's satisfaction.

5. Harmony

And when there is trust, there is harmony. There is no worry. No second guessing. Peace of mind. When you are confident that you have completed all the steps to good communication, your mind can relax and move on to other matters.

Good communication always includes follow-up to ensure there are no new concerns, glitches or questions.

You will be genuinely amazed by how much less confusing and simpler your life will be if you consistently practice good communication.

John paused momentarily and allowed Bob and Mary to absorb the information he had just given him. "Can you see how following these five simple steps could prevent unneeded confusion in your daily lives?" They both nodded in agreement.

"Good, we are in agreement then! To improve on the presentation of the five steps, we suggest you also keep the following nuances in mind."

Things to Consider:

Do not try to impress someone with how much you know by using uncommon technical terms or industry buzzwords.

Structure your conversation to the level of the other person's knowledge and understanding. Watch for blank stares, no input into the discussion, or questions being asked. Many people do not like to appear 'unwise' and, therefore, will not ask you to constantly explain what you mean. They will just stop talking. At this point, you have most likely lost your audience.

The Art of Listening

How many times have you heard or said – "That's not what you told me;" I didn't think it would cost that much," or "this is not what I ordered"?

What we have here is a failure to communicate! This happens every day. It happens in our workplace, personal life and throughout life in general.

It is ironic that in these days of instant communication – cell phones, internet and email – that lack of communication is still one of our biggest problems. The ability to communicate does not mean we actually communicate. In this world of 'hurry up,' our thoughts are going so fast we often hear without listening. We fail to understand what is required.

It happens on both sides of the conversation. Many people talk well but are terrible listeners. They never really hear what the other person is actually saying. If they begin agreeing to what you are saying before you are finished explaining it or finishing your sentences, you know it is their thoughts they are entering into the conversation (which may or may not carry the exact message you were conveying). When a person attempts to interrupt, you know they have finished listening and are now concentrating on what they wish to say.

At this point, you have a decision to make:

1. Ignore the interruption and talk louder

2. Let the person interrupt and deal with it

3. Acknowledge the interruption and return to your point

Ignoring the interruption solves nothing. Our minds are capable of only processing one thought at a time. If we attempt to continue talking, the other person will stop listening. They are trying to remember their ideas and are no longer paying attention.

If the interruption is relevant to your current point, sometimes it is better to deal with it. The person may require clarification or more information on something you have just said. Once you satisfy the person's need, you are able to continue with their full attention.

Should the interruption be irrelevant to the current topic or require a detailed discussion, it is sometimes best to acknowledge it. "That is a good question (valid point) and will be covered in the next segment (shortly, etc.)" or "that requires a separate discussion, let me make a note of that (or have the questionnaire make the note), and we will address it before the next break." Knowing their concern will be addressed, they can relax and give you their full attention.

To be a good communicator, you must present your ideas in a clear and organized manner and be a good listener.

John stopped talking for a moment and checked to make sure Bob and Mary were still engaged in what he was saying. After getting an agreement they were, John turned his attention to Bob and smiled.

"Without being gender insensitive, it is generally accepted that males may see things differently than females – especially colors. Do you agree, Bob?" How about you, Mary? Do you see colors differently than Bob?"

Mary grinned and glanced at Bob before turning her attention back to John. Bob lowered his head and gently shook it as if to say, "You have no idea how right you are, John!"

"Bob, if I were to ask you to describe the different shades of red to me, would it be fair to say your answers might be light red, bright red, regular red and dark red?"

Bob chuckled and acknowledged, "Yep, that would about cover it."

"And Mary, out of the 140 shades of red, might some of your answers include apple, crimson, burgundy, maroon or scarlet?" Mary nodded and laughed, "And some variations you might not even recognize!"

John continued, "To further illustrate this point on how an incomplete conversation can affect desired results, I offer you this example,"

What Color is Red?

A boss approaches an employee and says, "Here is a blank check. Go buy me a red vehicle".

Here is what could happen depending on the person's position within the company, level of authority, or personality type.

a) The salesman heads to a dealership and buys a new, fully loaded, candy-apple red convertible corvette. He drives around town for three hours, telling everyone <u>he</u> bought it for his boss.

b) The mother of four in safety buys a dark red utility van with sliding doors, removable seats, dual airbags and anti-lock brakes. She hopes to borrow it on weekends to take the family camping.

c) The shop supervisor buys a three-year-old, scraped, dented, faded red pickup truck with a lined box. He expects to use it to pick up parts and carry tools and supplies to and from the worksite.

d) The accountant knows what the company can afford. She spends all day trying to find a ten-year-old red sedan that has been reconditioned, is of good value, and still has lots of miles left on it.

The result is: Four different wants and needs, four different types of vehicles and four different shades of red.

Does the boss have any right to get upset with any of them? No! The boss did not even begin to practice good communication. Is this example an exaggeration? Yes, but only in the product used in the example, not the principle shown.

You would be surprised how often incomplete instructions are given. Some examples include office supplies/equipment, where to get vehicles fixed, delivery/pickup times or dates and on-the-job training. I am sure you can think of numerous other examples where you were not given all the required information.

The boss forgot to follow an essential step in good communication – filling in the details. He presumed that because he knew what he wanted, everyone else should also know. He failed to realize that every person has different experiences, wants, needs and skill levels. If you fail to fill in all the blanks, the other person will do so. They will either guess what you want or make a judgment call based on what they want, know or have experienced.

If you want a cherry red, four-door, 4.0 liter Ford Explorer with all leather bucket seats and a sun roof – say so!

Plus, also remember that communication works both ways. Practice being a good listener. Make sure you fully understand what the other person is trying to tell you. If you are a good communicator, you will quickly discover how much more enjoyable and uncomplicated your life will be.

Good communication is crucial to your success, whether in your business or personal life. How many people do you know that think – "I told them – I talked to them – I passed on the message" - is good communication? You now know differently. Remember:

1. Present your ideas

2. Make sure everyone understands

3. Ensure everyone agrees to what was agreed upon

4. Establish a level of trust between everyone involved

5. Enjoy the harmony that comes with **good communication**

John took a deep breath and leaned back in his chair. "I think that is enough information for this session. As we do at the end of every session, I am giving you a copy of what we covered today to put in your binders.

In the 'Selling' session, we will tell you how often people need to hear, read or experience something before remembering it. Therefore, we highly recommend you reread the material tonight and find someone to practice what you have learned with.

In our next session, we will cover a subject I know you will find very interesting – How to make a decision.

2. The Decision Making Process

What Should I Do?

Obviously, becoming more comfortable with the sessions, Mary and Bob were having a casual conversation when John entered the room. "Good Morning," he announced. "Did you review the material last night, and do you have any comments or suggestions?"

Mary spoke up, "Yes, we did. And then we went out to a new restaurant with some friends." I was so proud of Bob. There were times during the conversation when he couldn't clearly hear what was being said or did not fully understand what the speaker was saying. Bob would ask for them to repeat or clarify what was said. Our friends were impressed that Bob was actually listening and paying attention to what they were saying."

John smiled, "Well done, Bob!" The more you practice these techniques, the more you will notice your associates adopting them into their conversations.

You said you went to a new restaurant last night. Was that 'new' as in just opened or 'new' as to you had never been there before? See what I did there?

This topic easily segues into our next session – "decision making.'

Who decided on which restaurant to go to? Was it chosen for the style of food it served or because it was close to home? How did you choose what dishes to order? Did you decide what you really wanted or settled because of diet or health concerns?"

Was the decision made because everyone liked Italian food (emotion) or because your friends said it was inexpensive and had a good reputation (reason)?

True, these are small decisions we make in our everyday lives, but they still follow a succession of steps. Let me explain.

Many times, making a decision will come down to one of the following:

1. **Emotion and Rationalization**
2. **Reason and Logic**

A customer standing in the waiting area remarks, "It would be nice if there was a couch to sit on while I'm waiting." You think that is a good idea so you have a decision to make – do you:

1. Buy a couch and coffee table because it will make the customer happy or

2. Determine that wait times are usually relatively short and infrequent, so you get two padded dining room chairs and a small round table – at 1/3 the cost.

Although each is required in a successful company, they also have their respective places. Decisions made by **Emotion and Rationalization** are often more costly and less beneficial than those made by **Reason and Logic.**

Decision-Making Process

1. Gather Information
2. Listen to Advice
3. Review Pros/Cons
4. Make Tentative Decision
5. Take a Break
6. Implement Final Decision
7. Evaluate Results
8. Adjust as Required

1. Gather Information

Sooner or later, you will be required to make a decision that you might not have the direct knowledge to make a simple 'yes or no' answer to. When that happens, gather all the information you can – what are the details, who/what is it for, and when is the decision required?

2. Listen to Advice

Communicate with anyone who knows the situation – ask for input for suggestions or recommendations.

3. Review Pros/Cons

Make a list of the benefits and potential downsides for each possible choice. Take the time you need to make the right decision. A hurried, wrong decision can be expensive – not only in time wasted to fix it but also in additional costs or customer dissatisfaction.

4. Make a Tentative Decision

Review all the information you currently have. Is it enough to give an answer one way or the other? If not, then attempt to gather any missing information you require. If you feel you have enough input, then make a tentative decision.

5. Take a Break

If it is a tough decision that you are still uncomfortable with – take a break. Often, if you let your mind 'chew on it' for a while, the answers or new questions will present themselves.

6. Implement Final Decision

When you are satisfied that you are ready – make the decision and inform those who need to know.

7. Evaluate the Results

After a reasonable amount of time, do a follow-up with the person to whom the decision was given.

8. Adjust as Required

Were the desired results achieved? If not, adjust the decision as required. Continue doing follow-ups and reviews until the desired results are achieved.

Things to Consider:

Example #1 - A manager of a growing delivery company would like a new truck to show how successful (**emotion)** his company is becoming. When the driver tells him he has to return to the warehouse too many times to reload and that a larger truck would make him more efficient, the manager uses this to **rationalize** his emotional desires.

Investigation reveals that the truck driver finishes his current deliveries by 2:00 and hangs around the warehouse until quitting time. A larger truck would not increase his number of deliveries; it would only increase his nonproductive time. **Reason and logic** determine that a larger truck (and additional expense) is not warranted until the number of deliveries increases.

Example #2 - A company tends to exist with limited personnel during the early stages of startup. Many times, it is with only one or two people. They will do whatever **needs** to be done to make their company survive and hopefully become successful. It is not unusual for them to draft their own plans, visit the accountant/banker/lawyer, participate in the construction of their place of business, design their advertising, answer the phone, deliver the orders, write the invoices and do the bookkeeping.

Eventually, a business progresses to the point where there is not enough time to complete all the functions when they should be scheduled to be completed - deliveries are done during evenings and weekends, day-to-day bookkeeping deteriorates to become week-to-week bookkeeping, orders are missed because there is no one to answer the phone, follow-up on sales orders become less frequent – weariness and frustration set in resulting in **Emotion and Rationalization** dominating **Reason and Logic**. You need help, and you need it now.

The first personnel expansion of the company is now required. The owner(s) now have some decisions to make. Which responsibilities (functions) do they wish to release to another person's care? Who do they hire?

Do they hire the out-of-work, unskilled, unreliable relative (because they are available, it will keep the family happy and will work cheaply), or do they invest in a person with the required skill levels and fits in with the company's growth?

Emotion says: hire the relative – **Rationalization** says: I don't need a full-time person right now, but it will soothe the family, or I'll replace them as soon as I can afford someone with more skills.

Reason says: You need someone to reduce your workload and benefit the company. **Logic** says: Hire someone who will help solve your problem, not create new ones.

Which one do you think gets more often hired? Which one costs or saves you the most money (or headaches) in the long run?

Noticing Mary and Bob were still trying to fully absorb what he had told them, John added in a further footnote.

"Not every decision you make will require detailed analysis. Smaller choices may come down to experience, personal preference or necessity. Obviously, buying a new outfit or golf balls is a simpler decision than buying a new car or planning a new marketing campaign.

Point #3 above is where you must stop and ask yourself – am I doing this for the right reason?

Sometimes, the stars align, and the logical decision is also the one you really like!

As I will tell you at the end of every session, please reread the material and practice what you have learned today. On every decision you make, big or small, ask yourself – am I making this choice based on 'Emotion' or "Logic?"

In our next session, we will delve into 'The Management Process." It determines the goals you want to establish and the direction you want the company to take.

Of all the processes, this one will put your decision-making skills to the test. The good news is once you have completed these steps, you may only have to review your choices once or twice a year."

3. The Management Process

A Dream

"A dream written down with a date becomes a goal.

A goal broken down into steps becomes a plan.

A plan backed by action makes your dreams come true."

- Greg Reid

Where Are You Going?

John began the session by saying, "Someone once told me: If you don't know where you are going, how will you know when you get there?

When you go grocery shopping, do you know which store is your destination, or do you drive around until you see one that might suit your needs?

It is vacation time. Do you get in the car, pick the shortest route to a highway and drive until you run out of gas? Where are you going to stay? Did you pack the right clothes? Is there anything interesting to see or do?

If you only take a vacation once a year, you probably began planning it weeks or months in advance. You decided how much money you would be willing to spend. You check air flights or driving routes to get where you want to go. Accommodations would have been verified. The weather possibilities are a high priority on your list – you need to know what to pack. Your prime goal is to have a great vacation!

If you do all this for your vacation, why wouldn't you also do this for your business? After all, this is what pays for your holiday and the other niceties in life!

Do you know what a general description of a manager is? Their duties will include planning, organizing, staffing, leading and controlling the company's direction.

The management process sets goals and the direction your company will take to achieve them; it is the foundation for all the other processes. If you don't know where you are going or what you want to accomplish, no one else will either.

If you are starting a new business, this process will be more in-depth, take more time, and require more frequent reviews and adjustments to the objectives. Should you be taking over an existing company, many of these steps have already been taken and are in place. However, their vision may not be completely compatible with your goals.

Due to the gravity of this process, we will split it into two parts. The first sections will walk you through the steps to build the foundation of your company and get you started in the right direction.

The second part will help you decide what kind of manager you want to be.

To be successful, your staff and customers must buy into your vision. What will it be?

Management Process

1. **Set the goal**

2. **Establish the policies**

3. **Develop the procedures**

4. **Create the organization**

5. **Assign staff functions**

6. **Provide Motivation**

7. **Evaluate Results**

8. **Reset the Objectives**

1. Set the Goal

It's your company. You are now the boss! One of the first major decisions you must make is - What is your goal? What do you want your company to be known for? Innovation? Quality? Service? Price point? Your customers and staff will want to know your vision and how you plan to accomplish it. Using one or two sentences, write your goal down in simple and plain language. You may want to have both short and long-term goals. Examples might be:

To provide a quality product at a reasonable price

To increase sales by 10% by next year (specific)

Take your time. Do your research. Are your goals realistically achievable? Are they sustainable? Is there a labor force available? If sales increase, is there a supply chain for more products?

2. Establish the Policies

The definition of what a policy is: A policy is a set of rules or guidelines for your organization and employees to follow in order to achieve compliance. Policies answer questions about what employees do and why they do it.

How detailed and extensive your policies are may depend on the size of your operations. Policies include hours of operation/work, dress requirements, personal use of cell phones/internet, payroll procedures, and security. Templates and examples of company policies can be found on the internet.

This is one step you do not want to overlook or ignore. Not following safety standards, employment standards and various other rules and regulations can cause you a lot of grief if it comes down to your words versus theirs. Write your policies down and have your staff sign them to acknowledge they know, understand and agree to follow your guidelines.

3. Develop the procedures

A procedure is the instructions on how a policy is followed. How will it be done? Simple procedures might include what staff do when they start or finish their shifts, if they need to report an injury, or if a customer has a problem.

More complicated or involved procedures will require a detailed written set of instructions. Do not leave yourself open to malfunctions because the staff did not understand or forgot.

4. Create the Organization

Now that you have determined your company's purpose – Retail, manufacturing, repair/maintenance or a service provider – you need to create a list of the functions needed for each department in your business. Each of the following areas - accounting, sales, purchasing or marketing require their own list of functions to be done (See a more detailed explanation below).

5. Assign Staff Functions

Now you know what needs to be done, the question is, who will do what? Who is going to do the opening and closing? Purchase/make the product? Deal with the customers? Prepare financial records? In a small operation, a person may wear many hats and be responsible for different department functions.

An example would be the salesperson also making the deposit. The mechanic would also order the parts and supplies. Regardless of the staff size, the functions must still be done. See the following notes for more details.

6. Provide Motivation

How do you get them to do it? A paycheck is not always the only way to motivate someone. See #10, The Motivation Process.

7. Evaluate the Results

Nothing stays the same for very long. Every month or two, take the time to determine if you will need to re-evaluate some of the decisions you have made. Is the company growing faster or slower than you anticipated? Do you need to adjust your prices? Is your staff performing at the levels you expected? Do you need to make adjustments to some of your policies or procedures?

Evaluate your performance as well. Be honest! Don't let your ego get in the way of your business' success. What functions are you performing that bring you the least joy or causing you the most stress? Would you rather be building or fixing stuff rather than dealing with customers? Maybe you have an outgoing personality and would be much happier in sales or marketing than sitting in an office all day.

8. Reset the Objective

Nothing in the rules says you cannot fulfill a staff function and be a mechanic, baker, artist or salesperson. Hire or assign someone else to be the day-to-day operations manager. Assign them the roles you would prefer not to do, such as staffing issues, day-to-day problem-solving, and customer relations. Set their authority to a level you are comfortable with. Then, meet with them regularly (daily or weekly) for progress reports, to answer their questions or to provide additional instructions.

Changes can be challenging. They may affect staff or customer relationships. Unfortunately, that is also part of management. If you need to make a change – do it! If you made a mistake – own up to it! The important thing is to communicate this to your staff or customers. They may not like it, but they will respect your decisions.

See #6, Problem-Solving Process

John looked up from his material, leaned back in his chair and studied the two blank faces in front of him. In a soft, sympathetic tone, he said, "I know some of this is overwhelming, but there is also good news:

1. You only have to do this once and then review parts of it every six months or so.
2. There is lots of help on the internet to explain it in further detail.
3. In the beginning, it is unnecessary to produce a detailed fancy report. You do not have to do it all at once. Write out the basic points first and polish them later.
4. After you have gone through all the processes, many parts of this process will be much more apparent.

FUNCTIONS vs. PEOPLE

Let us expand on #5 above – Assign staff functions. What is a function?

51

Someone needs to open up in the morning, answer the phones, pay the bills or talk to the customers. These are 'Functions' (jobs) done daily and will be assigned to a member of your organization.

Of course, you want to feel good about the person you hire; you want them to be friendly, helpful and easy to get along with. But the bottom line is that you have a job (a function) that needs to be done and one that you want to be done effectively and efficiently.

The first step is to define the function and then assign someone with the skills to perform that function(s).

Example of functions:

Management	Admin	Sales	Shipping/ Receiving
Open Doors	Answer Phones	Prepare Mktg Materials	Receive Freight
Prepare for day	Prepare Deposits	Make Sales Calls	Count Inventory
Meet with Dept Heads	Reconcile Bank	Meet with Customers	Ship Sold Items
Solve Problems	Pay Bills	Fill Orders	
Deal with Prof. People	Collect Receivables	Update Media Info	
Develop Plans	Payroll		
Supervise Staff	Accounting		

This is only a small sample of the functions within your company.

The definition of the functions provides confidence and continuity (everything is being looked after), self-worth and organization (every person knows what they are responsible for and what is expected of them), harmony (discussions and decisions are based on the requirements of the function, not on the emotional attitudes of the personnel), and a vital management tool.

When planning is required or discussions occur, a manager can quickly identify where the functions fit into the company's organization and who should be involved. As you continue reading, you will discover how important identifying and assigning these functions are.

Things to Consider

If you are taking over an existing position (company), ask each employee to provide a list of everything they do, no matter how minor. They may give you strange looks, but tell them you are a rookie and need their help to be a better boss for them. Staff always like feeling more knowledgeable or smarter than the boss.

If yours is a Startup Company, your participation will be more involved. Should you have friends or associates that may do similar jobs, ask them for their assistance.

The more detailed the list, the better. Foremost, you want to ensure that everything gets done. Second, this will be a great benefit in the future for developing job descriptions and training purposes.

You don't want to get caught in a situation where you get told, "That is not in my job description" or "Nobody told me I had to do that."

Now that you have the list of what needs to be done, you need someone to do them.

As time progresses and the company' grows, people will get promoted, leave or share their responsibilities. However, the function always remains. It may change in priority, get modified, or be given to someone else, but the function still needs to be done.

In later sessions, we will cover the hiring and training processes. Your list of functions that need to be performed will be of great assistance during these stages.

Your company is now set up, and you are ready to take over being 'the boss' or the manager. Remember, you manage situations, not people. As a manager, your job is to ensure the functions are done correctly and efficiently by the person assigned to them. You will provide guidance, solve problems and provide support.

Management Style

What kind of manager will you be? There are many types of managers, including authoritarian, best friend, micro, missing, and open door/MWA,

Each management style has its own pros and cons. Everyone is different, and you will need to develop a comfortable and practical technique for you. Depending on the size of your staff and the complexity of your business, the odds are it will be a combination of styles.

How did you become a manager? Did you earn it through being qualified? Seniority? A relative? In the beginning, staff will respect your position, but they will judge you on your performance. Loyalty and respect for you need to be earned.

Authoritarian Manager

Not long ago, an 'Authoritarian' management style was the norm. Manager's kept their distance from the staff, and their attitude was 'my way or the highway.' Times have changed and are very seldom present in smaller businesses.

Sometimes, an employee is promoted from within the existing ranks of current employees. Their former peers will wonder how this will affect their relationships. They may test your leadership skills. Do NOT fall into the trap of being authoritative! This will backfire on you, may get you a reputation of being 'power hungry,' and your staff will distance themselves from you.

Instead, explain your new duties and responsibilities and request their help in accomplishing everyone's goals. Be Firm but Fair! Practice your leadership skills.

'Best Friend' Manager

The reverse is true for the one who wants to be one of the crew, the 'best friend' manager. If the staff does not respect the line between friendship and management, they may soon take advantage of the situation. They may stop following rules or procedures. This will undermine your authority, and production will suffer. Be friendly, but tell them where the line is – be Firm but Fair!

Missing Manager

Which is the most detrimental to your business (dept) – the micro-manager or the missing manager?

What is a 'missing manager'? Production, sales, administration or marketing employees may all work in the same or different areas of the building. Chances are the manager (boss) has their own office. Depending on the size of your operation, a manager may be responsible for many different functions, such as purchasing, sales or marketing. Many of their duties may require them to spend significant time in the office.

They may sit behind closed doors all day, and you only see them at meetings or when they arrive or leave. Staff are often left to work on their own for long periods without support or supervision. They are a missing manager. It will not take long for staff to conclude that if management doesn't care, neither will they. The quality of their work will decrease as their attention drifts onto personal interests – internet, cell phone, non-work conversations.

Micro-Manager

Micromanagers are the opposite. Not trusting or having the confidence in their staff to perform their functions to the manager's expectations, they go from project to project, inspecting every stage of production. Should the manager believe it is not being done to their standards, they will often inject themselves into the process and complete the task themselves.

This tends to demoralize the employees and affect their confidence in what they are doing. They will start to question their work and stop making decisions. Their productivity will go down. The more the employee questions their ability, the more the manager feels justified in micromanaging.

Maybe this is the style for you.

Open Door/MWA Manager

The last one we will discuss is the manager who believes in the open door/MWA management style. What is MWA? It is 'Management by Walking Around.' It is an amalgamation of different types that can produce numerous positive benefits.

Managers need to be seen. Depending on the size and nature of your business, visibility may be required only 3-4 times a day or as frequently as every hour.

If your business is small and you spend most of your time at your desk/work area, ensure the staff can see you. If your office has no window, leave the door open. It lets the staff know you are approachable. When you need privacy, close the door. Let the staff know you are unavailable during this time and to hold their questions until you reopen the door. They will soon respect this policy.

Suppose your business has multiple work areas (warehouse, production, retail, admin), and you cannot observe all the staff at the same time. In that case, you need to do a walkabout. Health experts will tell you that you need to give your eyes a rest or stretch your muscles at least every hour, so use that as an excuse if you must. Go fill your coffee. Check to see if a shipment has arrived. Ask sales if they have received a call back from a prospective client. If a project is underway, ask for an update. Ask questions!

Sometimes, you don't need to say anything. Don't hide (spy). Be in the open. Walk by their workstation. Watch from across the room. You would be surprised at what you can learn just by being observant. Are they on their cell phones, playing on the internet?

A disapproving look or a nod of approval can greatly improve an employee's performance. Staff needs to know and want to know that you appreciate their job performance.

Being readily available to answer questions, give advice, or offer solutions will go a long way in building a solid team.

Finding the right management style for you may take a while. Do not hesitate to adjust it as you gain confidence in your abilities.

Here are our final two points. If you are having a bad day, don't take it out on your staff – especially if they are not to blame. They will resent you for it. Lead by example, mix with the crew, and get your hands dirty occasionally. Your staff will appreciate it and will tend to follow your lead.

John took the last swallow of his now cold coffee. "We have given you much to think about in this session. Take some time to think about it. These steps do not have to be done all at once. Break the tasks down into smaller projects and take them one step at a time; it will be easier than you might think.

The important idea to take away from this session is that this process is the foundation for your business and what you will build everything else on. You will gain confidence in your decisions by taking the time and effort to do this now. You will feel comfortable in the direction your company is headed.

A final thought on this process for you. No one person can know everything. Never be shy in asking questions or seeking someone's advice or suggestions. Most solutions are achieved through a collaboration of ideas. People love to tell you what they know, and you will gain their respect by asking for their opinions.

Next time, we will work on the Leadership Process.

Management and leadership are often considered the same in many organizations. Though the two skills share similar traits, good managers are not necessarily good leaders. We will explain this in the next session.

4. The Leadership Process

Some time had passed since John had last met with Bob and Mary. "Welcome back! I thought maybe we had lost you for a while."

"Mary smiled, "No, we had a lot to think about, and we took the time to talk it over between ourselves and some business associates with whom we are friends. Bob's current boss also was very helpful. We are ready to proceed and are looking forward to the next processes."

"That's great," John replied. "I know that was a tough one, but I promise you it gets much easier from now on.

As I alluded to last time, we will be discussing Leadership today.

Being a manager and being a leader are not necessarily the same things! Sometimes, it is the same person but requires different skill sets.

The main difference between managers and leaders is that managers have people who work for them, and leaders have people who follow them.

The key difference is that a manager will focus on planning, organizing, giving direction, and coordinating projects to manage tasks and deliver results.

A leader will inspire, motivate, and influence those around them, which encourages people to achieve their goals.

Is Anyone Following You?

'If you are the leader, look behind you occasionally to ensure you are still being followed.'

Many managers are not good leaders. Managers can get caught up in the routine of running the 'business,' and they ignore their employees. Comments include, "I shouldn't have to babysit them; they know what they do, or I'm too busy to worry about petty stuff."

Employees, by nature, expect to be told when to arrive for work, what to do and when to go home. They hope to be mentored, encouraged and appreciated for what they do. Failing to receive validation, they may become disgruntled. They will follow orders but will do no extra. Their moral and performance levels will drop, and now you have a problem to solve.

The answer is to provide better leadership."

Leadership Process

1. Identify Need/Desire
2. Analyze Viability/Priority
3. Make Decision
4. Formulate Plan
5. Assign Responsibility
6. Provide Instruction/Training
7. Monitor Progress
8. Provide Guidance
9. Evaluate Results
10. Provide Feedback

1. Identify Need/Desire

By definition, as 'the boss,' you are the ultimate leader. But what if your business has multiple departments, more than one shift or is open seven days a week? If you try to do too much, you will suffer 'burnout' and become a less effective manager. You may want or need an assistant manager, a shop foreperson, a shift supervisor or a project leader.

2. Analyze Viability/Priority

Can you afford the extra cost? Do you need someone full-time, part-time or just for a particular project? Do you need to hire a new person, or can you utilize someone already on staff? Do you need them immediately, next week or when the company reaches certain sales or projection levels?

3. Make a Decision

Utilizing the steps in #2, The Decision Making Process, you can confidently progress to the next step.

4. Formulate a Plan

Did you decide to add an additional member to the staff? Maybe a more affordable and quicker option was temporarily promoting a current staff member to a working manager position. This option might be a compromise by reducing their regular workload and increasing their pay to cover the extra responsibilities.

5. Assign Responsibility

Decide which functions you will relinquish and assign to your new 'mini-boss.' Make a detailed list of this position's functions, duties and responsibilities. Refer to #1, The Communication Process, to ensure the staff member fully understands and agrees to what is required.

6. Provide Instruction/Training

This new leader is now an extension of you. If you want certain things done your way, make sure you impress upon them these details with precise instructions. If they have some flexibility in their leadership, you must also be aware of that. Follow the steps in #9, The Training Process.

7. Monitor Progress

How quickly the new leader adjusts to and becomes comfortable in their new position will largely depend on the complexity of the duties involved. Until you achieve confidence in their performance, regularly monitor how well they are doing. Don't hover, but be readily available if your assistance is required.

8. Provide Guidance

Initially, everyone getting used to a new position may feel nervous and unsure if they are performing to expectations. They may have a tendency to make errors or forget things. Take the time to meet with them and reinforce the areas they need to improve. Offer suggestions, tips and encouragement. Lead by example. Be a mentor!

9. Evaluate Results

After a reasonable amount of time, depending on the skill level of the position, it is time to evaluate your decision. Is the employee performing up to your expectations? Are they demonstrating the leadership

65

qualities you wanted? Are the staff accepting and listening to this person as a leader? Is this person reducing your workload and stress levels?

10. Provide Feedback

Lack of communication between management and staff is always a significant point of dissatisfaction. Everyone likes to know how they are doing.

Things to Consider

The next time you need someone to lead a project or want to be promoted to a leadership position, do a small test.

Pay attention the next time you are among a group of associates or out with friends. When someone (it might be you) says, "Why don't we... Or I think we should do it this way!"

Does the group agree or turn to another member for their opinion? Do they look to someone else for approval? They may not be the most knowledgeable or experienced person in the group, but this is who they believe will look out for them, who has their back and whom they trust. This is who we consider a 'natural' leader. They are usually outgoing and have good interpersonal skills.

"You will like our next session; I'm sure you will find it very beneficial. Everybody and every company will experience problems from time to time. We will show you the steps to quickly arrive at a solution."

5. Problem-Solving Process

How Can I Make It Right?

"Tell me, Mary, How many times does the power go out? Does your computer ever freeze or crash? Do employees ever claim there is a mistake on their paycheck?"

Mary nodded and replied, "All the time, John."

"How about you, Bob? Have you ever had a piece of machinery break down and been unable to get anyone to fix it? Have you ever had to delay production on a widget because a supply order was late?"

Bob gave a wry smile, "More often than we would like."

John continued, "Problems are an everyday occurrence in your life. Some will be a minor irritation, and others will require someone's time and expertise to fix.

The one problem many managers dread is dealing with an unhappy customer. If not handled satisfactorily, a minor complaint can escalate into a lost customer."

Reasons Why Companies Lose Customers

> 1% die
>
> 8% move out of the trading area
>
> 10% no longer need your product
>
> 14% no brand loyalty
>
> 67% poor service, customer dissatisfaction

While these percentages may vary in different industries and locations, they fairly represent a general statistic. Customers can be difficult to come by, and you don't want all your hard work destroyed by a less-than-helpful or inappropriate response. So, today, we will focus on how to dissolve an unhappy situation and turn it into a positive experience.

Are You a Problem Solver or Problem Creator?

Do you believe you are in business to make or sell a product and become financially secure? If you do, you are only partially correct. More importantly, you are in business to solve another person's problem.

I'm hungry - can you feed me?

I need this by tomorrow - can you help me?

I want a blue Whatzit – do you have one?

I have a question – can you answer it?

They have a problem. If you can solve it to their satisfaction, you have gained a customer!

On the other hand, if you:

Serve a meal with a hair in it

Are you late on your promised delivery date?

Did you give them a purple Whatzit instead of a blue one?

Give them incorrect information or attempt to bluff an answer

Now you or your staff are problem creators, and you may have just lost a customer!

Put yourself in their shoes. When you go into a restaurant for lunch, and it takes 45 minutes to get your meal, it is not how you ordered it or is not the quality you expected, do you really care that they are busy, rang in the order wrong or have a new cook? No! You had a problem – you were hungry, and they did not solve it to your satisfaction.

Now, instead of telling other people what a great restaurant it was, you tell everybody you met for the next three days what a lousy experience you had. You might forgive them once – it is a new restaurant – it has been excellent up to now – a busload of tourists caught them by surprise, and they were short-staffed. But if it happened again the next time you went in, how long would it be before you started looking for a new place to eat? If the trend continues, how long do you think before the restaurant loses a good portion of its business?

What should you do to make it right?

Problem-Solving Process

1. Identify Problem

2. Investigate

3. Develop Solution(s)

4. Allow Feedback

5. Implement Solution

6. Evaluate Result

7. Revisit the Problem

1. Identify the actual problem

The first thing to do is take a deep breath, relax and discover the problem. Is it a small problem, a big problem or possibly just an observation or a question? Get as many details as possible. Does it need an immediate course of action, or can it be put on a future agenda?

2. Investigate - Go to the Source

If the problem does not have a ready-made solution, then you go to the source of the issue. Talk to the machine operator who is having trouble. Call the supplier that cannot deliver. Talk to the unhappy customer. Listen to what the other person has to say. Be patient. Do not interrupt. Let the person tell you their story. Very often, a solution will be presented to you without you having to do anything.

Examples: The machine operator will tell you what part you need, where to get it and how soon he can be back in operation. The supplier may ship you a partial order until the rest is ready. The customer wants someone to know they have not been looked after to their expected level.

3. Develop a Solution

Once you know and understand the actual problem, you can begin to develop a solution to it. It may be no more than a quick decision, an apology or acceptance of a proposed solution. Other times, it may require a more detailed plan of attack. You may need to find a more reliable supplier, change a policy or procedure, or arrange compensation for the customer.

4. Allow Feedback

There is often more than one possible answer to any particular problem. Allow your associates or the persons involved to have input on your solution. Sometimes, slight adjustments or minor modifications to the first proposed solution will provide a more satisfactory result.

5. Implement Solution

Once a solution has been determined, put it into effect as quickly as possible. Remember the question – How long is a minute? It depends on which side of the bathroom door you are on! If you are the one solving the problem, five minutes can seem like five seconds. Five minutes can seem like an eternity for the person

71

in the situation. And with each passing moment, their dissatisfaction grows.

If the solution cannot be implemented immediately, then set a time frame for the situation to be resolved. Then, make sure you follow the progress. Good communication is essential to keeping any problem from escalating into a bigger one. Give and get progress reports. Make phone calls, write letters or email updates.

6. Evaluate Results

After a solution has been implemented, evaluate the result. Was it to the customer's satisfaction? Did it have the desired effect? Wait an appropriate time (depending on the severity or complexity of the situation) and call the customer, visit the machinist, or connect with the supplier. It will show genuine concern and sincerity on your part and will go a long way toward building future goodwill.

7. Revisit the Problem

Now is the time to investigate the cause of the problem. Was it just 'one of those things"? Is it a potentially recurring problem? Should a permanent change be made to a procedure or policy? Does someone require additional training? Problems can be costly - not only in lost customers but also in lost time and profits. Take the time to make the adjustments now, and you will increase customer/employee confidence and, at the same time, decrease your future stress levels.

Things to Consider:

It is remarkable how many companies continue to have the same problems over and over again. They are continually running around putting out fires rather than spending the time to find out what is causing them. Then they wonder why they are overworked, highly stressed, and the job is no longer fun.

Why do they let this happen?

1. Is their equipment overburdened or incapable of producing the desired results?

2. Are the materials used of lesser quality than expected or desired?

3. Are employees incompetent or improperly trained?

4. Is there a lack of direction, leadership or concern from the management?

5. Are their policies and procedures outdated or not enforced? Or even worse – they have no identifiable policies or practices.

How profitable can they be if they continually have slow service, ship incorrect products, have flaws in their product or the product does not perform as advertised? Take the time to identify the source of the problem and then solve it. Your customers, suppliers or staff will act or react to your leadership. If it is important to you, make it important to them because if it is not 'imperative to you,' it sure will not be 'imperative to them.'

Generally, most people do not like surprises. They want to deal with someone they can trust. It takes time and energy and requires a decision. They fear the unknown. Instead of solving their problem, you could be adding to it. As a result, when customers have a supplier, they tend to change them only when their issues are no longer solved.

Look at your own purchasing habits. Do you not tend to return to the same hairdresser/barber, the same mechanic, the same tax accountant or the same grocery store?

Sometimes, you will not be able to solve someone's problem. Never be afraid to say, "I am sorry I can't help you," or "I don't know." However, it should be immediately followed by "but I will find (recommend) someone who can" or "I will find out for you."

No supplier can have everything, and no person can know everything. Even if you can find a partial solution to their problem, the customer will remember how helpful you were and will most likely return with another problem you can solve.

If you want to be a problem solver, not a problem maker, then remember this:

If you promise to deliver – deliver what you promise!

It sounds elementary, but you would be surprised how many companies fail on this crucial point. The salesperson will commit the company to a time frame that production cannot meet. Companies will promote the biggest, the fastest, the cheapest or the best. Then, when you check it out, you find they have been less than truthful.

Have you ever gone to a sale that promises jeans at 50% off only to discover that it is just on sizes that only 3% of the population can wear? How about a grocery store that advertises butter at fifty cents a pound, and then you find out that you must buy six at the regular price first?

If you are expecting your purchase to show up on Monday and it does not show up until Thursday – if you want something in green and what you get is in red – if you thought it was going to be $30.00 and it turns out to be $49.00 – then you are not a happy camper and maybe no longer a customer. Look at things from your customer's point of view. The better you solve your customer's problems, the more successful you will be.

Nothing ever stays perfect for long. Equipment breaks down. Suppliers fail to deliver. People make mistakes. It happens, but what can you do about it?

People do not like problems, they do not like confrontations, and they do not like other people being upset at them. When some people hear, "Houston, we have a problem," they panic. "What will I do? We are behind schedule – the profit is lost – what will I tell the customer?". So what do they usually do? They tend to ignore the problem and hope it goes away. They can blow the issue out of proportion, get argumentative, become angry and release their hostilities on anyone nearby. They get defensive, proclaim their innocence and shift the blame elsewhere.

75

Unfortunately, none of this will solve the problem. When something goes wrong, it is important not to talk about who is to blame but who will fix it. Solve the problem first.

Additional Suggestions

If you are going to offer an apology – provide a sincere apology. "Sorry about that" just does not do. It is a quick answer that sounds as insincere as it is.

A customer is always right – even when they are wrong. They **believe** they are correct, and that is what is important to them and should also be important to you. Acknowledge their concerns. You can do this without admitting any wrongdoing on your company's part.

I.e., "I understand your concerns; now, what can we do to solve your problem?" You have now defused a possible confrontation or argument and emphasized a solution. Arguing over who is right or wrong will solve nothing. The customer wants to be satisfied, and you want a happy customer. Sometimes, letting customers 'be right' – even when they are wrong- greatly enhances your and your company's reputation.

Although you hope it never happens, there will be some customers you will never be able to appease. There may be outside influences to their actions – a boss with unrealistic expectations, an argument with a spouse, they are at the end of a bad day, or maybe they are just naturally belligerent, cranky and believe it's them versus the world. If this happens, you offer an apology the best you can, cancel their order, give them their money back, write off their bill and put it behind you. Do not dwell on it; let it continue to bother you or keep discussing it. Acknowledge the negative, learn from it, and move on to more positive areas.

Follow up

When a solution is not immediately available (a part needs to be ordered), keep in contact with the customer and provide timely updates.

You will receive bonus points from the customer if you follow up within a few days of an agreed solution to their problem. They will be calmer and may offer approval of the resolution or provide insight on how it could be handled better.

Either way, the customer will appreciate that you care about their satisfaction and remain loyal to your company.

Problems (customers) can be irritating and frustrating sometimes, but don't let a misunderstanding or mistake turn them away. Customers are your most valuable asset, and you should respect them as such.

6. The Project Process

What do You Want to Make?

Mary and Bob were all smiles when John joined them. Mary opened up the conversation, "That last session was quite informative. We can see where it will reduce emotional stress and lead to agreeable solutions."

John nodded in agreement. "That's great because it will help you in this following process.

The time will come when your daily routine will be interrupted by someone asking, "Can we.., will you.., how about we do..?

It's project time!

It may be simple, like planning a company barbeque, hanging Christmas decorations or organizing a staff birthday celebration. A new marketing campaign, designing or installing new equipment will be much more involved.

For the repeating or easier projects, you might get someone else to look after them. Others may require your direct input and supervision. Larger projects like marketing campaigns or renovations may require outside expertise.

The only thing you can be confident about is projects seldom go right the first time. There will always be issues or problems to solve, but now you know the steps to fix them.

How much easier would your life be if you could solve a problem before it becomes a problem?

Let's look at the way you can do this.

Project Process

1. Conceptual

2. Familiarization

3. Design It

4. Develop It

5. Review

6. Implementation

7. Follow-up

1. **Conceptual** (think about it)

   If there is one thing constant in our lives, it is change. Sooner or later, you will be presented with an idea to improve your operation. Maybe it will increase efficiency, enhance quality or increase profits. What should you do?

2. **Familiarization** (talk about it)

Do your research and become familiar with the subject. Discuss with the staff whose department or job may be affected by the idea's implementation. Make a list of pros and cons. Will it be time or cost-effective? Can it be implemented with existing staff, or is an outside source required? Should it be done now, or is it a project for later?

3. **Design It (lay it out) or plan it.**

Will the idea presentation benefit from a visual drawing?5678 A new web page, sales brochure, or workflow will be easier to understand if you can see it. Draft a rough sketch to highlight the main points. Do a time frame and cost analysis to implement the idea.

4. **Develop It (organize it)**

When the details have been worked out, and the feasibility or profitability of the project/product is ascertained and approved, the next step is **production.** Who will develop the product and the equipment or deliver the finished product or method? Will it be done by in-house personnel, an outside contractor or a collaboration of both?

5. **Review**

Who has the final approval before it is implemented? Have them review the completed design before it is implemented. Are the dates, prices or pictures correct? Is the quality of the finished product/equipment done to your specifications? Is the staff aware or trained for the new procedures?

6. Implementation

Once all the criteria have been met, pick a date for implementing the new system, equipment or method. Someone else may complete the tasks, but you are responsible for supervising it. There may be questions that need immediate answers.

7. Follow-up

The complexity of the project will determine how closely and often you need to monitor or follow up on the new situation. Never assume everything works right the first time. Check with staff or customers. Does it have the desired effect? Is it causing any unforeseen problems? Does it need any modifications?

Things to Consider:

These seven steps are cornerstones of any successful business. The startup of a new company will be your most significant project, but smaller ones should not be taken lightly.

Less than satisfactory results (or outright failure) occur because companies skip steps and go directly from the familiarization stage to the implementation stage.

Don't rush! Take your time. Missed steps and do-overs can be costly and time-consuming.

Give or get date commitments to/from project leaders when progress reports are due. Follow up on the due date. Reset the due date if necessary and then follow up again.

This is an excellent procedure to implement in weekly or monthly staff/department meetings. Assign special duties/functions they need to complete by the next meeting. It lets the staff know you are paying attention. They will tend to complete these projects much quicker than usual.

Remember the adage, 'If you don't have time to do it right the first time, when will you have time to do it over?'

John sat silent for a moment and then repeated the adage, "If you don't have time to do it right the first time, when will you have time to do it over?

Think of how many times you or someone you know has had to do something over again because they didn't read the directions, didn't recheck measurements, or monitored the work of the contractors. How much time or money was wasted because the job had to be redone?

Confident Bob and Mary had realized the importance of the point, John smiled and said,

"The day has finally arrived. It is time to open your doors and sell some products. How will you attract your potential customers? We will cover that in our next session, 'The Selling Process.'"

7. The Selling Process

How Many Do You Want?

"Tell me, Bob, how is the widget-making business doing? Is it running at full capacity, or could you increase production and sales?

Bob pondered the question for a moment. "The business is doing well, but I think if we reorganized the shop floor, added a new piece of equipment and expanded our product line, we could increase our sales by 25%."

Do you believe you can open the door, and the customers will walk in?

Selling Process

1. Attention
2. Need or Desire
3. Method
4. Action
5. Evaluate Results

1. Attention

If no one knows you have a product to sell, you obviously will not make many sales. To reach your potential customers, you first need to get their **attention**.

Why should they shop at your business? Is your product unique to your area? Do you have a convenient location? Is it available for a short time only?

2. Need or Desire

The context of your message should be designed to trigger an interest in your product/service. First, you must establish whether your customers '**need or desire** your product.

The average person does not care whether a toilet plunger is red or blue; they buy one because they need one. A golfer will buy a new suede golf bag with 14 zippered pockets, sonar, radar and an electronic ball finder if they believe they can knock 2 strokes off their game and look good at the same time.

Design your message so your customer perceives a benefit to them - not to you.

3. Method

What **method** should you use to get the information to your potential customers - personal contact, signs in the windows, flyers, radio or local paper? How about the internet, web pages, social media, clubs, and groups?

Very seldom does one way alone yield maximum results. Resistance to buy your product is considerably lower if the customer recognizes your name or product. (The most powerful selling tool you can produce is for your product to be recommended by satisfied customers.)

Analyze which methods are most cost-effective and productive for your company.

4. Action

Then take **action!** Develop primary and secondary campaigns. (eg. Direct mail followed up by personal contact). Develop name recognition through trade magazines/papers, trade shows or radio ads.

Join 'buy/sell' groups. Become a member of small business organizations, chamber of commerce or the Rotary Club.

Time your campaigns to coincide with your customer's most receptive time to buy. A Christmas toy (to dealers) sells best during September and October. Seeds and Fertilizer reach their high points during April and May. Personal contact yields higher results if preceded by a flyer/catalog a week prior.

5. Evaluate Results

This is most important! **Evaluate your results!**

Did the campaigns achieve their objectives? What could you have done better, differently or more effectively? Plan on spending 3-6% of your annual budget on promotions, advertising and marketing (6-8% is not unusual during the first two years). Advertising is not an expense; it is an investment.

During good times, you should advertise - during slow times, you **must** advertise!

Things to Consider:

If you are going to have a sale or promotion, think of your customer first!

Is this something your existing customers might buy on a whim? Will it induce new customers to try your business? Does the customer believe there is value to your offer?

Perception of the value of your offer will directly affect how successful your promotion or sale is. Be creative!

Instead of offering a 25% off sale, maybe reword the ad to read, 'Buy 1, get 50% off the second one. It costs you the same, but you have doubled your sales.

Everybody likes to beat the government. We have all seen successful promotions stating, 'We pay the taxes.' Depending on where you live, the sales tax could be between 5-12%. Of course, you still have to pay the taxes due, but the customer's perception is that they got one over on the government.

Don't try to put one over on your customers. Offering a 50% discount on dead stock or last year's inventory may not get their attention. Label the bin (racks) as clearance sale or inventory reduction.

Your goal is threefold: get people talking about your business, bring in new customers and increase sales. Think it through. What would convince YOU, as a customer, to visit your company?

John leaned back in his chair, "Well, did you find this session helpful?"

Mary quickly chimed in, "I already have several ideas running through my head!"

"Absolutely!" Bob nodded in agreement, "I now understand what we need to do."

"That's great," John answered. "Now that we have given you some ideas on increasing your business, how about we get you some staff to handle all those sales? That will be the subject of our next session."

8. The Hiring Process

Do you remember a job interview you once had? How did you find out about the position? Was it posted on the job site, on the internet, or recommended by a friend or associate?

How nervous were you trying to convince someone you didn't know that you were the right person for the job? Did they give you a fair opportunity to state your case? How long did you have to wait until you received their decision? Did you actually get a callback?

Hopefully, you do remember because now you will be sitting on the other side of the desk and asking all the questions. Don't worry; we have all the information you need to ensure you hire the right person.

When Can You Start?

The day will come when you need to hire a new employee. It might be to fill a new position or to replace a departing staff member. An entry position requiring minimum experience may be reasonably quick. A job requiring an experienced and skilled person will be more involved. Take your time! A hurried choice may end up complicating your life by creating mistakes, lowering the quality of your products and eating into your profits. A good choice will have the opposite effect.

Hiring Process

1. Identify Need

2. Develop Job Description

3. Advertise

4. Select qualified applicants

5. Interview

6. Evaluate

7. Re-interview

8. Hire

1. Identify Need

What do you want this person to do? Is it a new position? Will they be replacing someone who is leaving? What qualifications, experience, or skill levels are required? Are physical or personality traits necessary or beneficial to the work?

2. Develop Job Description.

When you clearly understand the job requirements, you must generate a job description for the prospective employee. It will include a list of functions (refer to #3, Management process) they must perform.

Each industry and position will have different requirements. An internet search for 'job description templates' will yield many free downloadable examples for you to choose from.

3. Advertise

The size or complexity of different industries may require various methods for finding the correct employee. An entry-level position in the service industry may only require a sign on the door or bulletin board. Social media may be the best choice should you need certified or experienced personnel. Local newspapers or employment offices are also viable alternatives.

Always list the applicant's required qualifications to reduce the number of frivolous applications. Specify if specific computer skills are required (i.e., Word, Excel). Ask for a handwritten cover letter if writing will be part of their job. Include a cutoff date for accepting applications. Add in how to submit their application (e.g., address, email, in person).

4. Select qualified applicants

Where you are located (city, small town, tourist destination) and necessary skill requirements may determine the response you receive from a few to dozens of applications. It may not be feasible to interview each one in person.

Depending on the size of your operation, it may be acceptable to have a department supervisor (chef, shop foreperson, office manager) read through each application to get an initial impression. Their experiences may notice small nuances you might miss.

Have them mark each applicant with an 'A' for 'Recommend to Interview.' Secondary options should be marked with a 'B,' meaning they are a possibility if no 'A' choices work out. Applicants obviously not suited for the position are to be marked with a 'C.'

When you are ready to begin the preliminary interviews, choose (3-5) from your 'A' group and set up an in-person interview (Zoom or FaceTime if that is acceptable). As a general rule, to avoid possible overlapping, you should allow 45 minutes to an hour between interviews.

If you are short of 'A' applicants, you might also shortlist a couple of 'B' applications. There might be a hidden gem in that group.

It is good business to let the remaining applicants know they have not been selected for personal interviews this time. They will appreciate your consideration, which frees them to consider other opportunities.

5. Interview

Each interview will be different. Less skilled positions may only need a short introduction meeting, and the decision may be made by only asking a few basic questions. In the service industry (server, cashier, sales assistant), personality may be more important than experience.

Higher skilled positions will require a more in-depth interview, sometimes more than one and with more than one interviewer.

The information provided by the applicant does not provide a complete picture. It is your company or department, and you should want your crew to work together effectively as a team. An outgoing, talkative individual may be desired for a server or salesperson but might be disruptive in an office environment or in production. You want someone who will 'fit in' with your company's atmosphere.

An interviewee may be nervous. Welcome them to your company and give them a short description of the job they are applying for. Confirm this is the position they are applying for.

Now is the time you want to find out who they are and evaluate whether they might be the one to fill the position. To help them relax, ask a few generic questions such as:

- Tell me something about yourself.
- How did you hear about this position?
- Why do you want to work here?

- Why did you decide to apply for this position?
- What is your greatest strength?
- What are your strengths and weaknesses?

When you are ready, dive deeper into their qualifications and consider asking:

- What courses have you taken or degrees/certificates do you hold?
- What specific knowledge or experiences do you have that would benefit our company?
- Have you worked with this equipment or in a similar environment before?
- Why did you leave your last job?

The last questions might produce standard answers, including the business closing or the lack of seniority in the downsizing or reorganizing the workforce. A motivating factor might be the chance for additional responsibilities or advancement at your company.

Note if the applicant becomes uncomfortable, gives a non-descript reply, or refuses to answer. This may or may not be a red flag. There may have been a personality conflict (not everyone always gets along) or dissatisfaction with the company or management direction. A change in their personal relationships may have prompted a shift in employment. If the applicant qualifies for a second interview, this question will need further investigation.

By now, you will most likely develop a positive or negative 'gut' feeling about this person. If the answer is negative, it is time to end the interview. If positive, you may want to give them more information about the company and discuss the details of the position.

The final stage of the interview might include the following:

- Give them a copy of the job description and answer any questions they may have.

- Now you are more informed about our company and the job, are you still interested?

- Are you aware of any reasons that might interfere with performing your duties to our company's standards, such as allergies, physical restrictions, childcare issues or commuting difficulties?

- Should you be chosen, when would you be able to start?

Conclude the interview by informing them when you will be shortlisting the applicants. Thank them for showing an interest in your company.

6. Evaluate

After completing all the interviews, it is time to evaluate your applications. Start with your top three picks. Call their references and ask the person to tell you about the applicant. Listen to their response. Are their answers straightforward, over-exuberant, or vague?

Unless they have asked you not to, call their previous employers. In these times of litigation, many employers will hesitate to give a previous employee a bad review. They are allowed to answer the question, "Would you rehire this person?"

The tone in their voice or reluctance to discuss this person's job performance may provide valuable insight.

Should there be another level of management between you and the position to be filled, consider inviting the manager to review your applicants for a second interview.

7. Re-interview

The second interview is to reaffirm your feelings from the first interview and to gain further insight into the applicant's suitability for the job.

Should the applicant be working under another manager, inviting them to join you in the interview is advisable. Should a technical skill be involved (mechanic, woodworking, computers), they can test the applicant's knowledge and skill more effectively than you.

At the end of the interviews, inform the applicant(s) when you will make the final decision and how you will let them know.

8. Hire

Decision day! Personally, call your selected choice and give them the good news. Give them any additional information they may require and determine a starting or orientation date.

Some positions may require certain conditions to be met or contracts signed before the actual starting date. Make arrangements for this to be done.

You may have had other applicants waiting anxiously for your decision. Now is the time to let them know the position is filled. Telling someone they were not hired 'this time' can be difficult, but if you were in their place, wouldn't you want to know?

Get ready for the new employee to join your crew. Have payroll assemble the employee package, including job description, benefits plan, and government payroll requirements. Inform the appropriate personnel that a new team member will be joining them.

Things to Consider:

During a business course I was attending, the instructor posed a question. "If a restaurant manager was going to hire a cook for her new restaurant, who would she hire (given that both had the same skill level and other things being equal)? Someone who had been a cook in the same restaurant for 16 years? Or – someone who had worked at eight different restaurants during the same 16 years?"

The answer is – the second applicant. Why? The first applicant did not have 16 years of experience. He had one year's experience 16 times. Most likely, he had worked with almost the same menu, the same equipment and the same procedures during this employment period.

However, the second applicant had worked with 8 different menus, 8 different kitchen layouts and equipment and 8 different managers. Odds were, the second applicant was more adaptable to change, had an increased knowledge base on menu selection and was a better problem solver.

Although the first cook might be more stable, the restaurant manager knew that during the startup of a new business, there would be growing pains, problems to solve, menus to develop and procedures to put in place. Being flexible was a key element.

Other employees may provide more value to your business if they have long-term experience (such as accounting staff) in one job. Weigh your options as to what is the most important to you.

On the first day on the Job

You must realize that most people are usually nervous on their first day. The new person will be lucky if they can remember their name. This is not a good time for intense training. Both you and your new employee will find it more beneficial if you only accomplish the following on the first day.

Tell them about your company.

    a) How long have you been in business

    b) What products/services do you make or sell

    c) Where is your main trading area

    d) Who the owner(s) is

    e) Who are the managers or the department heads

    f) Where do they fit into the organization

    g) What is the chain of command

    h) Who is their immediate supervisor

Get all the official paperwork completed.

    a) If you have a particular company application form, get it completed

    b) Payroll forms for tax deductions, etc.

    c) Any forms to receive company benefits – such as a medical plan

d) Explain how they fill out their time sheets/cards, where they turned them in and when

e) Tell them when the payroll cutoff is and when and how they get paid

f) Go over their job description with them and give them a copy

g) If you have company safety, operations, or procedure manuals, now is an excellent time to review them. Set a time frame as to when you want the new employee to have read and studied them.

h) Tell them about their training program and who will be doing the training, when and for how long.

Give them a tour

a) Where they should enter and exit the building (address emergency procedures)

b) Where they park their vehicle

c) Explain any opening, closing or security procedures

d) Where do they hang their coat or keep personal stuff

e) Where the washrooms are

f) Where they can eat lunch (when, for how long, refrigerator policies, how to work the microwave, etc.)

g) Where and how do they get supplies (both office and job)

h) Where their workstation/area will be

Introduce them

a) To coworkers

b) To their immediate supervisor

c) To the receptionist, accountant, sales manager (anyone they will interact with)

d) To the General Manager/Owner

e) Assign them a mentor or someone to help them through their first few days

Work on day one

a) Answer any questions they may have at this time.

b) Give them something easy or repetitious if you want them to be productive the first day.

c) Depending on the type of job they were hired to do, it may not be feasible or convenient to have them start their actual job part-way through the day. In this case, Schedule them to start the next day and then send them home early. This will allow them to absorb all the new information, relax, and prepare mentally to start fresh the next day. Trust me – they will appreciate it.

The new employee will be much more relaxed and comfortable on the second day. Therefore, the new employee will be more receptive to further information, and training will be more effective.

Depending on the size of your company, the above could take anywhere from fifteen minutes to four hours. Also, some jobs are more complex, and training times and programs will vary. You will have to adjust your needs or requirements accordingly. But remember, the first day on the job is still the first day on the job. The employee will want confirmation that they have made the right decision. They want to feel wanted and important to your company. When you take the time to welcome them and make them feel like an integral part of the team, the future rewards will far outweigh the inconvenience you experience.

The new employee will also be excited about starting a new job. They will tell everyone they know about it for a week. They have just become an unpaid salesperson for your company. As they will talk about you anyway, you might as well have them say what you want them to say about your company. You never know who they might know or talk to!

New employees will frequently want to assure you that you have made the right decision in hiring them and will be full of new ideas and suggestions on better ways of doing things – and they may or may not be correct.

You may have already tried some of the suggestions in the past or are already planning to make improvements in the future. Some of their ideas may be better and need to be investigated further.

If you are a progressive company, you always want to improve your efficiency or product. At the same time, this may not be the best time to discuss ideas or consider their merits. Most importantly, you do not want to dampen the creativity or enthusiasm of the new employee.

A good response might be to acknowledge their suggestion, thank them for their input and make arrangements to meet with them in a week or ten days to discuss their proposals (and make sure you do it). By then, they will be familiar with your current procedures and have weeded out the most frivolous ideas.

Should the idea be implemented, ensure the person gets credit for the idea/suggestion. If the procedure is involved, ask the person to join the meeting when it is first seriously discussed. This will build goodwill loyalty and, most importantly, induce the person to make more suggestions in the future (see follow-up under the leadership process).

We suggest you do a JPR (job performance review) after the first month. Tell them what you are happy/satisfied with their performance so far, and inform them of areas you would like to see improvement or work on. Get their view on their experience with the company and listen to any suggestions they may have.

Take notes and have them sign a copy as to what was discussed. * May be helpful for raises, promotions or terminations. Do a follow-up review in 3 months.

As a general rule, you should meet with each employee individually at least once a year (six months is preferred). Circumstances change. Attitudes change. Keep yourself informed. Solve a problem before it becomes a problem.

An Employee leaves voluntarily.

If there is one guarantee in the business, it is that one day, a valuable employee will quit. They may be moving, changing careers or (heaven forbid) finding a better job.

If they have given you proper notice of when they will be leaving, ask them to assist in transferring their responsibilities to a new employee. If someone has not been cross-trained in their position, would they be available to help in training when a new employee starts?

Is there an updated job description, with details, for their position?

Conduct an exit interview. Ask the employee why they are leaving and if they have any suggestions on improving their current job? Offer to write a reference letter if wanted. Wish them success in their future endeavors.

Don't let your disappointment in their leaving invoke a negative attitude. An employee who departs on good terms can be a goodwill ambassador and may benefit your company in the future.

You need to terminate an employee!

It is a day you hope never comes. Maybe sales or expectations have not been met expectations, nor improvements in efficiency mean you have to lay someone off.

The worst-case scenario is terminating an employee due to unsatisfactory performance. Maybe an attitude issue (square peg in a round hole) is causing moral problems with other staff. Outside lifestyles may be detrimental to your company's reputation. This is a nice way of saying everyone knows it is time for the employee to go.

The most challenging decision may be the employee who is doing OK but not great. Maybe they overstated their experience or knowledge, but they can't seem to perform to the required level of responsibility. Other employees are correcting needless errors or taking on additional duties to cover for them.

Suppose you have provided the employee with performance reviews, additional training and guidance without appreciable improvement. In that case, it is time to admit this person is not suitable for the job and let them go.

Steps to take

1. Review your area's labor standards, rules and regulations regarding severance or procedures.
2. To protect you and your company from any legal entanglements, we recommend that you have notes showing the steps you have taken to remedy the situation. Usually, 3 written reviews detailing meetings with the employee explaining the problems and

expected solutions are sufficient. These should be dated and signed by both you and the employee.

3. If the termination is immediate, have all the required paperwork (separation certificate, final pay) ready to give to the employee.

4. Have the meeting in a private area (your office).

5. It can be emotional on both sides. Keep the meeting short and on point. The decision has been made, and this is not the time for a discussion.

6. If the termination may be contentious (firing), it is recommended you have witnesses also attend the meeting. Get any keys, badges or company property from the employee and escort them off the premises.

7. It may be advisable to inform the staff the employee is no longer with the company. This will reduce rumors and gossip,

Taking away someone's security is tough, but the bottom line is sometimes it needs to be done. Take a deep breath and do it! Your staff and business will appreciate it!

What is your next step when you have changed your staff or reassigned duties?

Bob, do you remember your lesson from our first session?

It is the 'Training Process,' which we will cover in detail in our next session.

9. The Training Process

Tell me, and I forget

Teach me, and I remember

Involve me, and I learn

Benjamin Franklin

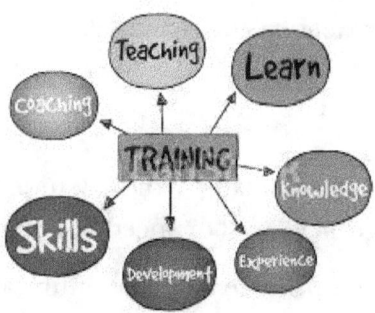

Let Me Show You How

Of all the processes and steps you take in life, this is the one that can significantly reduce or increase your stress levels and has a tremendous impact on how successful you are.

Then why do so many people spend so little time on it? Two reasons:

1. People naturally resist change. They want things to stay the way they are. They fear the unknown. They are afraid they will not understand or, even worse, appear foolish or unwise. As a result, they will resist you by offering all kinds of excuses --It will not work – It will take longer – the old way is better.

2. Most people do not like to teach or are uncomfortable doing so.

Why most people are not good teachers:

1. They have not been shown how to teach.

2. They do not fully understand what they are teaching and do not wish to appear foolish or not knowledgeable.

3. It takes time (which they never seem to have enough of)

4. They over-estimate the student's beginning knowledge, skill level or speed of learning

5. They do not practice good communication

As a result, they give information – they do not teach.

Training Process

1. **Tell them**
2. **Show them**
3. **Let them**
4. **Review**

1. Tell Them

Tell them what you want them to do. Be detailed and precise. Tell them the significance of what they are going to do. Tell them why they are doing it. Explain how it fits into the big picture. Follow the communication process – present the idea – make sure they understand and agree to what you have just told them.

2. Show Them

Once you have reviewed the verbal or written instructions, show them what they will do and how to do it. Do it **slowly**. Make sure they understand. Show them more than once if necessary.

3. Let Them

Now they know what to do and how to do it, let them do it. If feasible, let them do it three or four times. This will help them feel more comfortable doing it and give you confidence that they know how and are doing it correctly.

4. Review

If they appear to have difficulty in a particular area, go back to steps 1 & 2 and let them do it again. If everything is alright, let the trainee work alone and then return later for a progress report.

Things to Consider:

Implementing a change with the least resistance or possibly even enthusiasm requires some good old-fashioned hand-holding, clear, concise communication, and lots of

111

encouragement. Do this, and they will gain confidence in you, become more receptive to learning, and quickly adjust to a different way of doing things.

As mentioned previously, no one person can know everything. If someone else in your company or organization knows or understands the subject better than you, then have that person be the primary teacher, and you be the advisor or supervisor.

Before proceeding on this course, have a preliminary training session with the person doing the actual teaching/training. This is to ensure that they teach what you want to be taught. In effect, you are teaching the teacher.

Even if someone else is doing the actual training, attending some parts of the training sessions may still benefit you. Although it may produce some nervousness initially, it will increase the effectiveness of the training session.

The instructor will do a better job of demonstrating that you picked the right person for the job. The student will realize –

'If it is important to you, it had better be important to them.'

If the student appears intimidated by your presence, ask some simple questions (even if you already know the answers). This will help put the student at ease, is a good morale builder and shows you are human too.

At times, patience will become one of your most valuable assets. It is important not to show frustration towards or belittle the trainee. Calmness and encouragement will relax the trainee. It will be greatly appreciated and help build a stronger relationship between you.

If the trainee continues to have difficulties, take a break or switch to another task with which the employee may be more familiar. Sometimes, the light bulb takes a while to come on. Reduce the trainee's stress level and try again later.

Obviously, some training is more complicated than others. How to peel carrots can be taught in a few minutes. How to make good vegetable soup can take hours. In all cases, the four steps of the training process must be followed. The more involved the training program, the more frequent the follow-up and reviews should be. The trainee may have more questions or suggestions on improving the procedure.

Do a quick survey in your area – which businesses are the most successful, and which ones barely survive? Oddly, it is not necessarily the ones with the best or cheapest products that are the busiest. It is the ones who are the most consistent in delivering what they promise. They hire the right people for the right job and have excellent training programs.

Good training is not an expense; it is an investment in the future well-being of your company.

Cross-training

Being short-staffed is a common experience. What do you do when someone quits unexpectedly, goes on vacation or becomes ill? Are you covered for the short term? The answer is to cross-train your employees.

Naturally, the type and style of your business will determine the amount you can cross-train. Should you have a one-person office staff, you may have to delay most of the paperwork until they return. When you have two or more administration staff, you could also train the receptionist to make the deposits, open the mail or even do payroll.

To illustrate the point, consider a medium-sized restaurant where turnover is expected in day-to-day operations. Maybe you have a head server who has also been trained as a trainer (new servers) and produces the daily schedules of their department. Have them cross-train another server to also be a trainer (supervisor) and cover for them on their days off.

A busy family-style restaurant manager was asked, "Do you cook?"
"No," he replied.

"Well, what do you do if your chef is unavailable?"

The manager smiled confidently, "We have cross-trained the sous chef to cover for the chef. Then, we cross-trained the second cook in the sous chef's duties. Finally, we trained the dishwasher to work the line. Until I can find a replacement, all I have to do is wash dishes – and that I can do!"

It is not always possible to fully cross-train every position. Still, in most cases, you can provide short-term coverage until you can deliver a permanent solution. Cross-training staff can take time and effort, but it is an investment that will often pay off.

It should be noted that some employees will resist training someone to do their job. They may be concerned the trainee will do their job better and might replace them. Explain the benefits, such as the freedom to take time off. As an incentive, mention that they cannot get promoted unless someone else can do their job.

114

This goes for you as well. Free up your schedule by choosing a responsible employee and teaching them the opening and closing procedures. What other duties could be easily looked after while you are away or tied up on a project?

John looked up at Bob and Mary, "That is it! You now know how to hire and train your staff."

He turned and looked directly at Bob, "Soon, you will have some significant decisions to make and here is one I want you to think about.

You currently work in the production end of the company and obviously like what you are doing. Will you still enjoy it as much when management duties encroach on your time building widgets?

I have known many business owners who did not care to run their own businesses. Mechanics still wanted to be mechanics. Bakers preferred baking to being bookkeepers. Auto salespersons favored to continue selling cars. When their businesses grew to a size that they could no longer do what they enjoyed, they hired an operations manager to handle the day-to-day responsibilities.

I personally had that experience. A pub owner (bar, tavern) sold out and bought a restaurant. He was a terrific bartender and loved being on the front line with the customers. He did not have knowledge or experience running a kitchen, creating and designing food menus or developing marketing campaigns. So he hired me to run the business and the daily operations, and he worked the bar.

When he had questions or a major decision had to be made, we would go into the office, and he would sit on the owner's side of the desk. When the meeting was over, we returned to the public area, and he went back to bartending duties, and I was in charge again.

I'm not suggesting this is what you should do, but you might want to consider it in the future. Do what you enjoy and turn the other functions over to someone else. Meet regularly to ensure you are both in sync on the company's direction.

Now that we have set up your business, hired and trained your staff, and have a product to sell, there is only one more thing to address – how to motivate everyone on the team to perform up to your expectations.

10. The Motivation Process

Let me tempt you!

A key to any successful company is how motivated you and your staff are:

Motivated to show up each day

Inspired to do a good job day in and day out

Motivated to help your company grow and be profitable

What motivates people? Money? Of course. Fear? Sometimes. Actually, many things encourage people. A survey found that 'money' alone did not make the top five reasons that motivated them at work. If you want someone to perform, you need to take the time to find out what motivates them. It may not be just one reason, but one will be more important than the others. In no particular order, here are five possible motivations.

Motivation Process

1. Food & Shelter
2. Security
3. Social Acceptance
4. Status
5. Achievement

1. Food and Shelter

If you do not have anywhere to live and cannot afford to eat, you are not a happy camper. Generally, the more you make, the nicer the place you live and the better you eat. When considering your business for employment, applicants will always ask themselves – "Can I afford to work here? Can I pay my rent? Pay my bills?" Self-survival is a major key to motivation.

2. Security

Is it full-time? Is the company going to be around for a long time? Is there a benefits package? Is there a retirement plan? Many people want to know (if they do a good job) that you and they are in it for the long term. It allows them to plan a family or buy a home. They will invest more time and energy in their job and will be more willing to upgrade their skill levels. They will often begin work at a lower starting wage if they believe the job is secure.

3. Social Acceptance

Life can be challenging. We all like encouragement and acknowledgment that we made a good decision or are doing well. Ask a person where they work or what they do, and then watch their response. You will quickly discover if they are proud of the company they work for or the job they do.

4. Status

Why did garbage men become sanitation engineers? Housewives – homemakers? Truck drivers – expediters? Very simply, because it sounds better and less disrespectful.

5. Achievement

Other than points 1-4 above, people will join your organization because they believe you will help them climb the ladder in their chosen careers. They will become an apprentice to achieve the goal of being a journeyman. Many chefs started out as line cooks.

Laborers become carpenters and electricians. A data entry person graduates as a business manager.

Maybe your place of business cannot directly help them on their chosen path, but you can provide the underlying support they need. For example, they are from out of town but move here to go to college or trade school. Your employment opportunity satisfies all the items on the list. It is a valuable asset to them.

"Your most important assets aren't your clients; its your loyal employees. If you take care of your employees, they will take care of your clients."

Things to Consider:

Let us end this session with a story.

A new restaurant was opening in town. A few days before the opening, the manager summoned all the newly hired staff for a meeting and training session. After his welcoming speech, he asked each person to stand up and state their name and what position they would be filling.

Starting with the front-end staff, everyone he pointed to stood up and introduced themselves. Next was the kitchen staff. He was almost done when he spotted a shy teenager doing his best to hide behind a post. "And who might you be," he asked? In a low voice, the young fellow replied, "I'm James, and I'm just the dishwasher."

"Now, just a minute," the manager interrupted! With every eye following him, the manager crossed the room and stood beside the young lad. Raising his voice slightly so everyone would hear him, he declared, "No, you are not just a dishwasher!"

Startled, James slouched and looked down at the floor. The manager paused to let his words sink in. Then he smiled and warmly said, "James, you have the most important job in the restaurant!"

Bewildered, James looked up at the manager and asked, "What do you mean?"

The manager glanced at the kitchen staff, "It doesn't matter how good the food looks or tastes." Shifting his focus to the front-end personnel, he said, "It doesn't matter how good your service is. None of it matters if there is dried food on the cutlery or china – the customer's experience is ruined."

Turning his attention back to James, the manager continued, "So, you see, James, our success depends on you. You are not 'just a dishwasher,' you are a 'kitchen specialist! Welcome to the team!" As the staff cheered and gave James a round of applause, he stood tall and proud to be there.

That evening, the manager printed off business cards for each staff member and added one particular word to the end of their job titles. At the next training session, in front of everyone, he handed James his business cards. They read: James Smith – Kitchen Specialist Extraordinaire!

Over the next many months, James became cross-trained as a prep cook, 2nd cook, and server. It was not long until he was promoted and turned his job over to the next 'kitchen specialist.' All because someone knew how to be a motivator!

Final Thoughts

This material has provided plenty of good information to put you on and keep you on the right track to 'Be the Better Boss.'

What are you going to do with it?

Some people say, 'There was some good stuff in there," and then put it on a shelf or in a drawer and never look at it again. They soon forget most of what they learned and wonder why they repeatedly solve the same problems.

Other people will keep it handy and refer to it when utilizing one of the 'Processes' and want a refresher on what steps they should take.

Do you remember the first time you sat behind the wheel of a car and took your first driving lesson? Remember how awkward that felt and how nervous you were. I bet you hardly even think about it today – you just get in and drive.

The same will happen with running your business – take the time to learn and practice these processes now, and soon, they too will become second nature, and you will do them automatically without thinking about them.

Over the years, I have worked for, with, and observed numerous different management types. I have noticed that untrained, undisciplined or authoritarian managers generally tend to achieve a much lower success rate. On the other hand, managers who are consistent in their 'firm but fair' management style, show respect to their staff and take care of their customer's needs tend to have a much higher rate of success.

Your success level will depend on how much effort you put into it!

What kind of boss will you be? You now have the knowledge to be a very good one. The choice is yours! I wish you all the success you deserve!

Things to Consider:

How much time you have depends on how big the emergency is – a small investment in time at the beginning will save you much time and frustration later on.

Old commercial warning– You can pay me now or pay me later.

If you do not have time to do it right the first time, when will you have time to do it over.

Be like Santa – check your list twice.

John pushed back his chair, stood up and extended his hand to Bob and Mary.

"Thank You for spending your time with us. I have a good feeling you will have great success in your new adventure.

A final point to remember: No one person can do everything. Utilize support from your staff, family and friends. Don't be just the boss – be a team leader! The dividends will be well worth the extra effort!

Knowledge by itself is not power – it is the use of knowledge that makes you successful!

If this material has been of value to you, please recommend this book to someone who may benefit from it and become **'The Better Boss."**

Bonus Tips for Successful Management

- Be fair – Don't play favorites
- Be consistent
- Respect fellow Management/Staff
- Be a good listener
- Admit your mistakes
- Teach – do not just tell
- Solve problems before they become problems
- Solve issues promptly and efficiently
- Practice good communication
- Do not presume/assume
- Do not procrastinate
- Request – Do not demand
- Show Appreciation
- Give informative feedback
- Deliver what you promise
- Stay organized – plan ahead
- Learn to Delegate – (Monkey Management)
- Be firm but fair!
- Say 'Good Morning' and 'Good Night'
- Smile more!

Printable Process Sheets

For your convenience and quick reference guide:

Please print the following Process sheets and keep them in/on your desk or tape them to the office wall.

Download them to your tablet, computer or phone.

COMMUNICATION PROCESS

PRESENT IDEA

UNDERSTANDING

AGREEMENT

TRUST

HARMONY

DECISION-MAKING PROCESS

GATHER INFORMATION

LISTEN TO ADVICE

REVIEW PROS/CONS

MAKE TENTATIVE DECISION

TAKE A BREAK

IMPLEMENT FINAL DECISION

EVALUATE RESULTS

ADJUST AS REQUIRED

MANAGEMENT PROCESS

SET THE GOALS

ESTABLISH THE POLICIES

DEVELOP THE PROCEDURES

CREATE THE ORGANIZATION

ASSIGN STAFF FUNCTIONS

PROVIDE MOTIVATION

EVALUATE RESULTS

RESET THE OBJECTIVES

LEADERSHIP PROCESS

IDENTIFY NEED/DESIRE

ANALYZE VIABILITY/PRIORITY

MAKE DECISION

FORMULATE PLAN

ASSIGN RESPONSIBILITY

PROVIDE INSTRUCTION/TRAINING

MONITOR PROGRESS

PROVIDE GUIDANCE

EVALUATE RESULTS

PROVIDE FEEDBACK

PROBLEM-SOLVING PROCESS

IDENTIFY PROBLEM

INVESTIGATE

DEVELOP SOLUTION(S)

ALLOW FEEDBACK

IMPLEMENT SOLUTION

EVALUATE RESULT

REVISIT THE PROBLEM

PROJECT PROCESS

CONCEPTUAL

FAMILIARIZATION

DESIGN IT

DEVELOP IT

REVIEW

IMPLEMENTATION

FOLLOW-UP

SELLING PROCESS

ATTENTION

NEED & DESIRE

METHOD

ACTION

EVALUATE

THE HIRING PROCESS

IDENTIFY NEED

DEVELOP JOB DESCRIPTION

ADVERTISE

SELECT QUALIFIED APPLICANTS

INTERVIEW

EVALUATE

RE-INTERVIEW

HIRE

TRAINING PROCESS

TELL THEM

SHOW THEM

LET THEM

REVIEW

MOTIVATION PROCESS

FOOD & SHELTER

SECURITY

SOCIAL ACCEPTANCE

STATUS

ACHIEVEMENT